How to Officiate
Weddings and Funerals

By Pastor Jeff Culver

DEDICATION:

To my wife, who inspired me to write.

**ISBN: 9781522028901
Imprint: Independently published**

May God's blessing be upon you as
you serve His people in both their joys
and their sorrows.

How to Perform a Wedding Ceremony

MY BACKGROUND AND REASONS FOR WRITING

Introduction of Author

I have been in the full-time ministry for 21 years, and have served as a Senior Pastor since May of 1998. Ministry has brought my wife, Kathryn, and I to some of the most amazing places in the United States, places that many people vacation at, yet we have had the privilege to live there. Having raised our two boys, Dion and Stefan, we are now learning how to live with an empty nest.

I began my full-time ministry journey at Lake City Assembly of God in Medical Lake, WA, just outside of Spokane as their youth pastor. It was here that I learned the foundation that I would build my ministry style and ideals upon. After serving about two years as a youth pastor, I felt the call of

God to venture into the pulpit, not knowing what awaited me.

Angoon Assembly of God in Angoon, AK would be the church that I would be my first senior pastorate, and it was here that I quickly realized that what I had learned in Bible School had not fully prepared me for the major life events, such as wedding and funerals, that I would now be fully responsible for. Angoon is in one of the most beautiful parts of the world, Southeast Alaska, and the Tlingit people are even more wonderful than the scenery that is found along the famous Inside Passage. It was here that I officiated my first wedding and performed my first funeral. This church was so gracious with this new pastor and I will be forever grateful to them.

After three and a half years, I had felt a very distinct leading of God to move to another church, and shortly thereafter found myself pastoring Dillingham Assembly of God in Dillingham, AK. Dillingham is found in Western Alaska on the north end of Bristol Bay, and is traditionally the home of Yupik Eskimo people, though the community itself is now very multi-cultural in its makeup. Three years later, after perhaps the most profound experience with God that I have ever had, I was called to the state of Minnesota.

Moving to Minnesota was quite an adventure for my 2 boys, my wife, my dog and myself. We had to fly our four-wheel drive club cab pickup truck with my snowmobile in the back of it from Dillingham to Anchorage on a C-130, where the ultimate horror story began. You have heard of airlines losing luggage, but how do you lose a four-wheel drive truck with a snowmobile in the back? Dillingham insisted they flew it to Anchorage while Anchorage insisted it was still in Dillingham. After a few hours, they thankfully located our truck in Anchorage and we were able to begin the long drive to Detroit Lakes, MN.

Detroit Lakes, MN, located about 45 minutes west of Fargo, ND (which is nothing like it is depicted in the movie, Fargo), and is known as a major part of Minnesota Lakes Country, and a popular vacation destination, is where we would spend the next 11 years of our lives, pastoring the wonderful people of Detroit Lakes Assembly of God. Here, we were immersed in yet another very distinct culture, the Scandinavian culture of the Upper Midwest.

After our children graduated from high school and were in college and beginning their own lives, the Lord moved on us again to relocate to another strange and exotic land where we find ourselves ministering today, on St. Croix in the US Virgin Islands, from Alaska to a tropical paradise. The vast majority of the members of our congregation are not native to St. Croix, but come from the many different island-nations that make up the Lesser Antilles.

Occasion for Writing

As you can see, our ministry has been very unique in that we have lived and ministered in a variety of very different cultures, each of which have very different sets of cultural expectations and very different approaches to major life events such as weddings, funerals and just about any other event that can be imagined. I have conducted weddings in each of these different cultures, and while styles and ceremonial differences certainly arise, the core process of conducting a wedding is quite consistent across culture.

I remember vividly the first time I was asked to officiate a wedding, I had really, very little training in the matter practically. Yes, I had, like all ministry students, completed a couple of courses in pastoral studies which covered weddings, funerals and the like, and even had to purchase some Minister's Handbooks as part of my textbooks, but having a set of various wedding and funeral services in my possession and actually performing the ceremony are two very different things. At that moment, I realized I had absolutely no idea what to actually do. I could write a paper on weddings and funerals, I could pass quizzes and tests on them, but to actually do one? I realized that I was going to have to learn on the fly.

It is this difference between the classroom study of weddings and funerals and the officiating of these very important life events, and the sacred duty of the minister to respect, honor and fulfill his or her role in a manner that contributes to the memories of these milestone days. Since we should be only performing one wedding and one funeral for each person, we want that positive experience to last a lifetime.

This is why I am writing this brief guide, so that those who are just entering the ministry can have a practical guide on how to perform wedding in an organized, professional manner that blesses the bride, groom, their families and the many other people involved in a wedding for a lifetime.

THE WEDDING PROCESS BEGINS

A Long Process

The wedding process is a long process. The wise minister will quickly recognize that most, but not all, couples that have come to point of marriage have begun their journey together long before the minister is involved in their relationship. Perhaps they have been dating for a year or even longer. It is not uncommon today to see couples that have remained in the dating process for several years before arriving at the desire to marry. They have already gone through many of the ups and downs that a marriage will have to endure to stand the test of time. They have both been angry with the other and also had their hearts filled with pride to the bursting point. They have developed a unique culture of their own that they now desire to last a lifetime.

The question, that question filled with the greatest of hopes and at the same time the greatest of fears has been asked, "Will you marry me?" The affirmative response then leads the couple to the minister. This is a pivotal moment in the planning of the wedding ceremony, and should never be casually agreed to over the phone, but an appointment should be scheduled to have a brief meeting.

The First Meeting

The importance of the first meeting with the bride and groom cannot be overstated. This is why I advise to always schedule this meeting in your office of place of ministry, and to allow around 30 minutes for this meeting. In this meeting, several things should occur that will lay the foundation for everything that will follow. Remember, to make this memorable for this couple and their families, communication is vital.

The first event that should occur is an assessment of the relationship between the minister and the prospective couple. Ask yourself if you know them well, if not, take a few minutes and introduce yourself and ask a few general questions about them, where they were raised, what they do for a living, general questions that ease the tension. If you do know them well, particularly if they are members of your church or close friends, ask how they are doing and if they are having a good day. Taking a few minutes to break the tension will make for better communication, for tension is there with the importance of the events to be discussed, and in the long term, a better overall experience for all involved.

After these few minutes, I suggest a brief prayer asking for God's guidance in the meeting, and then ask them how you can help them, which opens the doors for them to ask you officially to officiate their wedding. It is at this point you officially accept the invitation and take the next step to schedule the date and the location. It is important to have a long-term planner available to you to write dates and times like this down, for the wedding process often begins months, even up to a year before the event itself. The church needs to be reserved for such a date, you need to keep your calendar clear, for it seems often there will be an opportunity for another event on the day scheduled, and this is an event you do not want to double-book.

After agreeing upon a date and location, the next step is to schedule pre-marital counseling and following that, dates to actually plan the ceremony.

The Importance of Pre-Marital Counseling

The importance of pre-marital counseling cannot be understated. I got married to my wife Kathryn in 1991. We were two fairly new Christians who didn't know much of anything but we knew that we wanted to be a whole lot more than just friends, we wanted to make a life together. Like many other young couples of our day, we simply contacted our pastor, who agreed to do the ceremony, gave us brief ceremony preparation and Bam! We were married and headed into the great unknown with absolutely no idea what lay ahead and no idea of the tools we needed to handle what lay ahead. By the grace of God, we are still married, but we had to learn so much the hard way.

Marriage is not always an easy road filled with romantic dinners and midnight walks on the beach. It is often a battleground, and marriages that have been grounded with pre-marital counseling have such a better chance of survival in today's world.

The world-renown Mayo Clinic defines pre-marital counseling in this way, "Premarital counseling is a type of therapy that helps couples prepare for marriage. Premarital counseling can help ensure that you and your partner have a strong, healthy relationship — giving you a better chance for a stable and satisfying marriage. Premarital counseling can also help you identify weaknesses that could become problems during marriage.[1]"

Elisabeth Joy LaMotte notes that "It is so easy to get carried away with meaningless but pressing details such as which cake flavor to choose, what floral arrangement works best and whether to send out save-the-date notifications. Pre-Marital Counseling can help couples keep their priorities grounded and focused on what the wedding preparations represent — the decision to build a life together.[2]" There are so many details that need to be planned in a wedding, it is easy to let the details blind a couple to the more important realities that lie beyond the day of the ceremony. Don't let couples neglect the importance of the lifetime they are planning to spend together. I personally will not perform a marriage that does not involve pre-marital counseling, as I have become convinced it is even more important than the license itself.

Some states are now beginning to recognize the importance of pre-marital counseling in the planning phase of a wedding and offer greatly discounted, or in the case of Texas, free marriage licenses for those who have successfully completed varying lengths of pre-marital counseling. Since I spent several years pastoring in Minnesota, and Minnesota is one of the states that offers a significant cost reduction of a marriage license, I will look for a moment at their policies.

"In August 2001, the State of Minnesota enacted a bill regarding premarital education. This bill offers a $75 waiver off marriage license fees to couples who complete a minimum of 12 hours of premarital education that includes a premarital inventory and the teaching of communication & conflict management skills[3]." I believe that

Minnesota's law is the most aggressive of the seven states offering this pre-marital counseling discount, but while ministering there I became convinced of its intrinsic value.

My Pre-Marital Counseling Plan

There are many different resources available to a minister today on the topic of marriage preparation, pre-marital counseling and wedding planning. I think it is good to become familiar with many different perspectives, that you will have a wide variety of information to draw upon during the pre-marital counseling sessions. While it is good to have this vast difference in perspectives available for easy reference, I think at the same time it is good to not overload the prospective bride and groom with too much information. They simply won't be able to take it all in. By the time they reach the pre-marital sessions, they are in full-planning mode, so I focus on that which will bring them the most benefit long-term.

I begin my pre-marital counseling sessions twelve to fourteen weeks before the actual ceremony. Because I pastored in Minnesota for so many years and Minnesota requires a 12-week pre-marital counseling program, I have created a 12-week process. This longer period gives me and the couple many meetings in which to clearly communicate their desires and dreams for their wedding day, and me to offer any suggestions which I feel will enhance their experience or answer any questions that may arise during the process. I focus the most on self-disclosure and communication skills. My experience has been that most marital conflict is communication-based and that learning to clearly communicate and trust that what your spouse-to-be states about their feelings is true to the best of their ability is not only the best form of conflict resolution but of conflict avoidance as well.

To this end, the first four sessions are based upon what I believe to be the four big areas of communication issues, which can be major issues of mis-communication and contention. I have written the first four weeks of my pre-marital counseling worksheets, which I hand to both the bride and the groom. In each of the 45-minute counseling sessions, I always have a few minutes of greeting to break any tension, followed by prayer, and then a brief introduction of the topic of the day. I try not to spend more than 10-15 minutes in this coaching session, but move on to my instructions on how to use each worksheet.

I emphasize that they are not to bring back their completed worksheets to me, but are to fill them out separately and then meet together to go over what the other has written in response to each question. This self-disclosure often brings a great deal of clarity to issues that are often not clearly defined before marriage. When we meet the following week to begin work on the next topic, I ask them simply if they found the session enlightening and if it brought clarity to the subject, and I am almost always responded to in an enthusiastic "yes!"

I have included the four worksheets in an appendix in the back and encourage you to copy them and use them for yourself, just please keep the copywrite information on them and do not sell them. The following are the first four weeks titles.

1. The Big Dream

2. Clarification of Roles

3. Financial Practices

4. Expression of Love

Beginning the fifth session, I begin to move on towards the actual planning of the event along with the first of two outside sources that have proved invaluable to thousands of couples over the years. I will cover the planning of the wedding ceremony in the next section, so I will not address that now.

The next four weeks of counseling revolve around Gary Chapman's classic book, "*The 5 Love Languages*". This is a book I believe every couple should read and re-read many times over the course of a marriage. It is good for the bride and the groom to purchase their own copies, yet read and study the contents together. Over the course of these four weeks, I simply ask questions regarding the insights they are discovering. It is exciting to watch couples light up as they discover new things about their soon-to-be spouse, or finally understand why he or she is "that way". More information and many other resources that might be of use to you can be found on this website, http://www.5lovelanguages.com/.

The last four weeks of the counseling portion I center upon a DVD series by Jimmy Evans entitled *"Our Secret Paradise"*. This DVD series deals with romantic and intimate love and while this is an issue that needs to be discussed between the two, I do not feel it is really appropriate for the minister to be informed of their intimate desires.   This series is a powerful series Biblically based and clearly

presented. Jimmy and Karen Evans have an

abundance of wonderful materials regarding dating,

marriage, strengthening your marriage, and

restoring your marriage that I highly recommend.

More can be found at their ministry's website,

http://marriagetoday.com.

PLANNING THE WEDDING CEREMONY

Materials Needed for Preparation

As I stated above, I begin the actual planning of the wedding ceremony at the fifth pre-marital counseling session. One of the reasons that I do this is that it is helpful to engage couples in the counseling process and keep them engaged through to the end of the process. Because they have so many things on their plate at this point, most of which are focused on a specific date on the calendar, it is so easy for them to let the homework go by the wayside. Incorporating the planning process into the counseling process allows for ministerial accountability and keeps them involved in the process through to the end. Ultimately, my goal is not only for them to have a wonderful wedding day, but also a wonderful marriage.

To plan a wedding ceremony, the most important book needed is a minister's handbook. I am an Assemblies of God minister, and our denominational publishing company, Gospel Publishing House makes these available at a low cost. Many other denominational publishing companies do so as well, and there are countless other resources for various wedding ceremonies that can be found at a Christian bookstore or online outlet such as Amazon.com or Christian Book Distributors.

Beginning the Process

I initiate the process of planning the wedding by asking the couple about their dreams for their big day. I pay careful attention to their answer, making both mental and physical notes that will help me facilitate their dreams to the best of my ability. I pay careful attention to major desires, is it a traditional wedding, a casual wedding, a beach or outdoor wedding? Differing styles and venues require a different sort of presentation, and the minister's presentation is a big part of the ceremony, so I take this time to learn their desires and make the necessary adjustments to meet their needs. Paying careful attention to the many couples whose weddings I have officiated has led me to many different settings and a lot of different attire.

There are still many that desire a traditional wedding. While suits and ministers are not seen together as often as in years gone by, it is still important to have one or two well-fitting suits for these occasions, and funerals as well. I have worn suits to weddings, but also have worn a pair of khakis and a simple button-down shirt to others, and even a pair of blue jeans and a flannel shirt. Whatever they desire, dress that way, don't make your clothing an issue.

After determining the style of wedding, formal or informal and the corresponding venue, church or outdoors, you are then better prepared to suggest certain wedding ceremonies. I always print off several different wedding ceremonies for couples before this meeting, and at this point I hand the copies to them, and tell them to read each one of them, and see which they like best. I don't stop there, however. I encourage them to feel free to mix and match different portions of different weddings. Above all, I encourage them to express themselves and their core values in their ceremony.

This comes from my own wedding experience, a day I still cherish more than words could ever express. We got married outside by a lake, and I wrote and recorded all of the music for our day, the groom's entry, bridal party process, bride's entry, recessional, the whole thing. We played it on a tape player placed prominently near the place where we exchanged vows. The ceremony still, nearly 26 years ago at this writing, means so much to me I want to encourage others to make their own special memories as well on their special day.

With this stack of ceremonies to read and the story above to encourage them to be creative, I let them go. Along with the first few chapters of "The 5 Languages of Love", this will be more than enough homework for a busy couple.

The Pieces Come Together

The weeks pass quickly in the process of putting together a wedding ceremony, and the planning of the ceremony itself comes together fairly quickly. When they come back to meet for the sixth week, they often have already picked out the ceremony that they prefer. I always offer a wide variety of ceremonies for couples to choose from, but have found that well over 50% choose the same ceremony, the shortest ceremony I have. Most tend to tell me just stay with the ceremony of their choice and add nothing to it while some add a vow they have written.

After they have presented me with their choice, I ask about the other details involving the ceremony. Do they want the bride and groom to stand on the traditional sides, groom to the right and bride to the left? Is there music picked out yet, if so, what is it? Is there going to be a special singer or a special song, if so, I find out the song and the singer, as well as when they want to put that in the program. I recommend only one special song during the ceremony itself, and suggest all others can better be placed at a reception afterwards. Most if not all couples I have worked with have thought that to be good advice and followed it to their pleasure.

The other details at this meeting to ask are if they want some form of unity ceremony in their wedding ceremony. Many have asked for a unity candle, unity sand, a unity rope or even a unity painting. While not all couples want this, it is very important to those who do, and I usually suggest placing these immediately after the saying of the vows and the exchanging of rings.

In the seventh and eight counseling sessions, I use a few minutes of each session to finalize the program and get all the details in order and on paper. This keeps communication clear and helps me to fulfill my role in this big event well. At this point, with the wedding between four to six weeks away, it is important to have the outline of the ceremony close to a finished product.

The final four weeks of counseling and planning sessions revolve around the DVD series I assign and the multitude of last-minute questions that inevitably will come up. It seems that there is always one issue or another that will arise that needs a solution. Most of all, as the day is drawing near, reassure the couple that in the end, it will work out and the day will be one of the most special days of their entire lives. Be positive and encouraging most of all in the final few meetings.

THE DAY BEFORE THE WEDDING

The Rehearsal

The day before the wedding is an important day, and the rehearsal is an important moment, as all of the months of planning are now going to be put to the test. This dry run will make sure everything works smoothly during the big event.

Often, weddings will occur on a Friday or Saturday. Most weddings I've been involved in occur on a Saturday. The rehearsal then happens the night before. It is important to remember that in many cases, the wedding rehearsal is not the only item on the evening's agenda, as many people also schedule Bachelor/Bachelorette parties as well. Even if they do not have such a party in mind, it is still important to be prompt and not keep the wedding party too long. I try to schedule rehearsals to begin at 6:30pm if at all possible, that way everyone can be on their way no later than 8:00pm.

Make sure you arrive at the venue at least 30 minutes earlier than everyone else so that you can meet the arriving wedding party fully prepared, and recorded copies of the processional, bridal march and recessional already loaded and ready to play. This sets a professional tone that sets everyone at ease. Have a joyful attitude, while maintaining a professional demeanor. As soon as the party is arrived, organize them immediately.

After giving them a succinct overview of expectations and the ceremony's plans, start by making sure everyone has a printed copy of the order of ceremony, and each member of the wedding party knows who they are marching in with. Line this group up first and demonstrate how they are to walk in, be it casually or formally. Next, direct the bride and her father to their locations behind the wedding party and lastly place the groom at the beginning of the procession. Most of the time the groom has walked in with the minister.

After you have lined the party up, quickly begin the first practice. Proceed through the entrance and when everyone is properly placed, stop and make sure everyone felt comfortable with the entrance, if not, address any issues. Next, go through the giving away of the bride and the positioning of bride and groom for the vows. Making sure everyone is comfortable with the process, proceed through the vows and ring exchange. Have then pretend to light any unity candle or other unity item, then proceed. The only part I withhold is the kissing of the bride, I think that can wait one more day. Move on to the recessional.

Keep the mood lively and the rehearsal moving quickly. While not rushing things, do not allow for dead spaces, keep the flow going so people do not become distracted and lose interest. After the first walk-through, ask if there were any questions and address any issues or concerns. If the ceremony went well, simply practice the procession and recession one more time and then show people where they can get dressed. I have found that showing them the rooms set aside, particularly for the bride and bridesmaid is better shown after the rehearsal for practicalities sake. Dismiss the party and allow them to proceed with their evening.

THE WEDDING DAY
Before the Ceremony

Arrive early to maximize your preparation. I try to arrive at least one hour before anyone else so that I can read the vows on more time and make sure I am comfortable with my part of the program. This also allows for any last-minute changes that need to be incorporated as the result of the rehearsal the night before.

As the wedding party arrives, make sure to greet each member and direct them to their staging areas. Make sure all of their needs are taken care of, the personal touch goes a long way on the wedding day. I always remind them to be at the staging area ten minutes prior to the announced starting time. This helps with punctuality and general organization. At this time, I collect the wedding license. I cannot perform the wedding with no license.

I learned the importance of collecting the license before, not after the ceremony the hard way one time. I asked for the license and they had not acquired on yet. That was a mess, so get the license before the ceremony.

Five minutes before the announced start of the ceremony, I make sure the bride is ready, usually by asking the Maid of Honor to confirm this for me. If she is ready, I inform her that we are about to start so that she can proceed to her staging area. I then join the rest of the wedding party and make sure they are all ready, followed by a short prayer. The final task is to inform the musicians and sound technician that it is time to begin.

With the first notes of the processional sounding, I begin the entrance. Over the course of the ceremony, I always keep in mind that while I, the minister, am a large part of the ceremony, the ceremony is not about me. It is about a man and a woman pledging before God Almighty, surrounded by friends and family, that they from this day forward will live as man and wife until death parts them. Everything I do is mindful of the fact that this day is about these two people, they are the stars, the reason everyone has gathered.

Paperwork

After guiding the ceremony through to its conclusion, proceed immediately, along with the Best Man, the Maid of Honor, bride and groom, along with the photographer to the office area for the signing of the license. Do not forget this part or delay it. Make sure all signatures are in their proper places, distribute the newly married couple's copy to them along with the copy they must file with the state, and take your copy as well. You need to keep this copy on file, so I usually go right to my office and file it.

Finally, go through the reception line, congratulate the bride and groom and then search out every member of the wedding party and thank them for their contribution. Many times, some members will be unchurched and every opportunity to insert yourself into their lives can create an opportunity to share Jesus Christ and His saving grace with them. Take this time to meet as many people as you can, for you never know when an opportunity will arise for future ministry.

I pray that this short guide will help you as you prepare officiate a wedding. May God's richest blessings be upon you in Jesus name.

APPENDIX

Pre-Marital Worksheet 1: The Big Dream

Understand that your revelation is only part of the greater whole.

Focus on your connection points:

Define your roles based upon your gift packages.

    1. Self-define your gifts

    2. Self-define both the strengths and weaknesses of these gifts

What does your future spouse view as your

strongest gifts?

Scripture study: Eph. 5:22-33

Pre-Marital Worksheet 2: Clarify Your Roles

Understand that your background, your family experiences, your experiential learning of gender roles are now only half of the equation. Two experiences, two histories are now merging into one new history that will not be like either person's experience up to this point.

It is very important to emphasis the similarities in your experience to this point. Similarities are the points of agreement that will form the foundation of your family.

Describe your experiences in a family. Include decision-making processes, discipline, child-rearing, household chores and any division of labor there,

1. What was the Husband's role?

2. What was the Wife's role?

3. As they grew, what were the children's roles?

What did you like about each role?

1. Husband's role:

2. Wife's role:

3. Children's age-progressive roles:

What did you not like about each role?

1. Husband's role:

2. Wife's role:

3. Children's age progressive roles:

Looking again at Eph. 5:22-33, how does this passage of Scripture impact the forming of your definitions as a couple?

Pre-Marital Worksheet 3 – Financial Practices

"The Buck Stops Here" Who do you think the final decision, the husband or the wife or by consensus, regarding major financial decisions?

Are you carrying any outstanding debt into this marriage? If so, what are your current payments and what is the outstanding balance? Include such things as credit cards, lines of credit, car loans, housing mortgage, student loans/college debt and any other indebtedness.

1.
2.
3.
4.
5.

Are any of these debts outstanding or facing collection? Are there any garnishments or judgments against you currently?

What are your attitudes towards debt?

What are your attitudes towards savings and investments?

Are you bringing a savings account, investments or a retirement account into this marriage? If so, discuss honestly your opinions and intentions regarding merging these accounts or keeping them separate.

Are you bringing any real or titled property into this marriage? If so, discuss what property you are bringing and if it is going to be kept separate, merged or sold.

Pre- Marital Worksheet 4 -Expressions of Love

Gary Chapman identifies 5 expressions of giving and receiving love, which he calls "Love Languages". The first language is affirmation, next is gifts, then acts of service, quality time, and lastly physical touch.

According to Chapman, we demonstrate love in our primary love language, hoping to receive the same in return. Reality is that rarely if ever do two people entering a marriage speak the same "love language". Therefore, it is vitally important to learn your spouse-to-be's language of love so that you can accurately express your feelings of love and appreciation to the other in a way that will be received.

Rank in order the following expressions of love in the order of importance, 1 being the highest and 5 the lowest. Affirmation, gifts, acts of service, quality time and physical touch.
1.
2.
3.
4.
5.

How does your list compare to your spouse-to-be's list? Is there a great difference or are they fairly close?

Where is your primary language on your partner's list?

Communication as how specifically to speak the other's language of love is very important, it doesn't just happen.

Ask the question, "How can I effectively speak your language of love?" Record the answer below.

Purpose in your heart to regularly and intentionally communicate love to your spouse-to-be from this point forward in their self-defined love language.

BIBLIOGRAPHY

1. Mayo Clinic Staff. (2014, November 25). Premarital counseling. Retrieved June 05, 2017, from http://www.mayoclinic.org/tests-procedures/premarital-counseling/basics/definition/PRC-20013242

2. LaMotte, E., LICSW. (2014, April 22). A Case for Pre-Marital Counseling. Retrieved June 05, 2017, from http://www.huffingtonpost.com/elisabeth-joy-lamotte-licsw/a-case-for-premarital-counseling_b_5185620.html

3. Minnesota Premarital Education Bill. (2015, January 06). Retrieved June 05, 2017, from http://omf.stcdio.org/marriage-ministries/marriage-preparation/marriage-preparation-resources-for-clergy/minnesotal-premarital-education-bill/

How to Officiate a Funeral

MY BACKGROUND AND REASONS FOR WRITING

Introduction of Author

I have been in the full-time ministry for 21 years, and have served as a Senior Pastor since May of 1998. Ministry has brought my wife, Kathryn, and I to some of the most amazing places in the United States, places that many people vacation at, yet we have had the privilege to live there. Having raised our two boys, Dion and Stefan, we are now learning how to live with an empty nest.

I began my full-time ministry journey at Lake City Assembly of God in Medical Lake, WA, just outside of Spokane as their youth pastor. It was here that I learned the foundation that I would build my ministry style and ideals upon. After serving about two years as a youth pastor, I felt the call of

God to venture into the pulpit, not knowing what awaited me.

Angoon Assembly of God in Angoon, AK would be the church that I would be my first senior pastorate, and it was here that I quickly realized that what I had learned in Bible School had not fully prepared me for the major life events, such as wedding and funerals, that I would now be fully responsible for. Angoon is in one of the most beautiful parts of the world, Southeast Alaska, and the Tlingit people are even more wonderful than the scenery that is found along the famous Inside Passage. It was here that I officiated my first wedding and performed my first funeral. This church was so gracious with this new pastor and I will be forever grateful to them.

After three and a half years, I had felt a very distinct leading of God to move to another church, and shortly thereafter found myself pastoring Dillingham Assembly of God in Dillingham, AK. Dillingham is found in Western Alaska on the north end of Bristol Bay, and is traditionally the home of Yupik Eskimo people, though the community itself is now very multi-cultural in its makeup. Three years later, after perhaps the most profound experience with God that I have ever had, I was called to the state of Minnesota.

Moving to Minnesota was quite an adventure for my 2 boys, my wife, my dog and myself. We had to fly our four-wheel drive club cab pickup truck with my snowmobile in the back of it from Dillingham to Anchorage on a C-130, where the ultimate horror story began. You have heard of airlines losing luggage, but how do you lose a four-wheel drive truck with a snowmobile in the back? Dillingham insisted they flew it to Anchorage while Anchorage insisted it was still in Dillingham. After a few hours, they thankfully located our truck in Anchorage and we were able to begin the long drive to Detroit Lakes, MN.

Detroit Lakes, MN, located about 45 minutes west of Fargo, ND (which is nothing like it is depicted in the movie, Fargo), and is known as a major part of Minnesota Lakes Country, and a popular vacation destination, is where we would spend the next 11 years of our lives, pastoring the wonderful people of Detroit Lakes Assembly of God. Here, we were immersed in yet another very distinct culture, the Scandinavian culture of the Upper Midwest.

After our children graduated from high school and were in college and beginning their own lives, the Lord moved on us again to relocate to another foreign and exotic land where we find ourselves ministering today, on St. Croix in the US Virgin Islands, from Alaska to a tropical paradise. The vast majority of the members of our congregation are not native to St. Croix, but come from the many different island-nations that make up the Lesser Antilles.

Occasion for Writing

As you can see, our ministry has been very unique in that we have lived and ministered in a variety of very different cultures, each of which have very different sets of cultural expectations and very different approaches to major life events such as weddings, funerals and just about any other event that can be imagined. I have conducted many funerals, far to many to count anymore in these different cultures, and while styles and ceremonial differences certainly arise, the core process of conducting a funeral is quite consistent across culture.

I remember my first funerals, I had really, very little training in the matter practically. Yes, I had, like all ministry students, completed a couple of courses in pastoral studies which covered weddings, funerals and the like, and even had to purchase some Minister's Handbooks as part of my textbooks, but having a set of various wedding and funeral services in my possession and actually officiating such a solemn ceremony are two very different things. At that moment, I realized I had absolutely no idea what to actually do. I could write a paper on weddings and funerals, I could pass quizzes and tests on them, but to officiate do one? Having no one to ask, and having no "how to" book available, I realized that I was going to have to learn on the fly.

It is this difference between the classroom study of weddings and funerals and the officiating of these very important life events, and the sacred duty of the minister to respect, honor and fulfill his or her role in a manner that contributes to the memories of these milestone days. Since we should be only performing one wedding and one funeral for each person, we want that positive experience to last a lifetime.

This is why I am writing this brief guide, so that those who are just entering the ministry can have a practical guide on how to officiate a funeral in an organized, professional manner that blesses those who are left behind, family, friends and close associates, and at the same time reminds all who hear that there is an eternal destination awaiting at the end of this life. May they all choose well where they will spend eternity.

The Moment of Death

Death is inevitable, it is part of the cycle of life. In the death and dying process, the minister is often called upon to play a major part. To new ministers, this can be a daunting process. When in your youth, your 20's or early 30's, death seems so foreign, so distant, and to be asked to be with a family as an elder passes from this life unto the next can be filled with awkwardness.

I can clearly remember walking into that Bureau of Indian Affairs home, perhaps ten homes down the road from my own. It was dimly light, family and friends gathered in the small living room and there, on the couch, lay her body. They had called me that she was passing and I rushed to the home, but while I was in transit she had passed. Family cried, and reached down and touched her hair one last time. Cancer had claimed another victim far too young.

This was my first direct experience with death as a minister. No amount of classroom lectures and presentations could prepare me for the real thing. I felt awkward, completely out of touch with the moment and inwardly wanted to run. I could not run however, and in a short while was asked to pray for the family, which I did and shortly after my prayer the medical staff arrived to remove the body. I had begun the journey towards my first funeral. I went home, completely drained, and I couldn't get the scene out of my mind.

In this guide, I will be discussing how to meet with the family, interactions with the funeral home, memorial services, various types of funeral sermons, the day of the funeral, the graveside service and interaction with the various people and personalities that will all be involved in the process of a funeral.

The Meeting with the Family

After the death, the body is turned over to a funeral home for preparation. Depending on the cause of death, this can be very quickly or it can take some time. Usually, after two to four days, a funeral director will contact you and schedule a meeting with the family members, usually at a funeral home office, though I have conducted many of these meetings in my own office as well. It is in this meeting that the process of putting together the funeral will begin. Before you go into this meeting, you need to have an understanding of what information you need to properly plan a funeral. At the end of this book will be a sample order of service to refer to.

The purpose of this meeting is to obtain any last wishes of the deceased, the families wishes, an accurate portrayal of who they were, arrange a memorial service if desired, confirm a date and time of the funeral service, discuss the graveside service, work out any family conflict (which unfortunately is often the case as conflicting desires arise), and prepare an order of service. I will briefly cover each of these below.

The Deceased's Last Wishes

It is not uncommon for people who know that death is imminent to make requests as to their funeral. Perhaps they left a few of their favorite scriptures or a favorite hymn they would like sung. Be very careful to include these requests, because this is their final self-expression and it is important to honor these requests if at all possible. I recognize that not all requests are practical, but make every effort to accommodate these requests.

The Wishes of the Family

This is, in my opinion, the most important factor of all factors involved in the death process and funeral arrangements. I have always attempted to make the most concessions in the arraignment of the funeral to the immediate family, that is, spouse, parents, children of the deceased. The funeral is not for the dead, but the living, and it is primarily for those who lived with and loved the one who has passed.

If the family has a strong Christian heritage, they will often ask for a funeral sermon on a specific topic, which I make an effort to accommodate. The reason I do so is that the most requested topic I have heard is a request for a salvation message. I will discuss the topic of sermons later on in this book.

Families will also request to have other ministers say a few words, perhaps a special song, or congregational singing. Pay very careful attention and take detailed notes as you hear the wishes of the family. Always get the phone number of the family spokesman, and keep all communication with him or her, because too many voices create a chaotic funeral.

Order of Service

Another very important outcome of the family meeting is the establishment of an order of service. A sample order of service is found at the back of this book. You want to establish primarily who will give the opening prayer, who will lead the songs, who will give the eulogy and any family statement if desires, and who will sing the special song.

By way of experience, if there is another minister the family would like to put on the program, the opening prayer and the closing prayer are the best places to place them. It is important to give them a place however, as they have played an important role somewhere in the families lives.

An Accurate Portrayal

If the deceased was a member of your church, this is a rather simple task, as you more than likely know some if not most of their immediate family and there is a degree of relationship to draw upon. If this is the case, volunteer some major characteristics and life events and ask if you can use these in your sermon as illustrations. The family will appreciate your suggestions, and it will often prime their memories to a favorite moment they may request instead. Take accurate notes if you are not familiar with the event. These are very important pieces of your funeral message.

For example, while I was pastoring in Detroit Lakes, MN, an elderly lady who was so full of life passed away at an old age. She had been a nurse during World War Two, and I had officiated her husband's funeral a couple of years earlier. He had marched in FDR's funeral procession in Washington D.C. near the end of the war. She was proud of her and her husband's service to their country and loved God with everything that she was. These were important events, and I included them in her funeral. There were two other things about her, however, that were keys to making this funeral represent her accurately; her heart for reaching the lost, and her sense of humor, which was a hallmark of her personality.

Knowing this, and knowing that she had shown me a picture of her in Las Vegas at a slot machine, she laughed often about the picture, for she never gambled a day in her life, and some relatives tricked her into that photo. They got her good and she appreciated a good "gotcha!" So, I requested the family if I could share that picture, and form my message around the phrase, "Don't Gamble with Your Soul." They loved it, because it combined her passion for the lost and her huge sense of humor. Look for these keys to form the central points of your sermon.

You will, however, also be asked to officiate funerals of people you did not ever meet in their lifetime. This will usually be because they were not Christians, but had a relationship of some form with one or more members of your congregation. Often times, these initial meetings will be a first-time meeting between you and representatives of their family. These meetings are extremely important not only for the funeral but also to establish a relationship with unsaved people.

I have officiated several funerals of people I did not know. In these cases, key characteristics of the deceased and spiritual background are extremely important. Let me give you a couple of examples.

In one case, I was asked to officiate the funeral of a teacher who had a tragic boating accident and died immediately. His family was from the Midwest, and talking to the father and his two brothers at the front of the church while he smoked a cigarette, I asked him why he had asked me to officiate the funeral. He told me that he was raised in my denomination and while they were backslidden, his own words, he felt loyal to the denomination. This was an important key for me to frame my sermon around.

The second thing I learned from this conversation was that the son who had passed was "spiritual", though not religious. This was also an important point for me to see how I needed to approach the funeral message.

In another case that recently occurred, less than six months ago at the time of this writing, I was approached by a recent convert at our church to officiate the funeral of a cousin of hers. Here in the Caribbean, known for its beaches and sunshine, cruise ships and tourism, is a dark secret. It is also a place of violence and criminal activity. On the island I live on, there is an ongoing gang war, west side vs. east side. He was a west side member, and was the target of an east side hit, due to his alleged participation in violent activity.

So, what I had was a church full of gang members and in the coffin a murdered gang member. Taking all this into consideration, I simply appealed to the young men and young women that they didn't have to walk the path to the end that this young man did. Before and after the service I made every effort to meet these young men and form some sort of rapport with them, that perhaps I can be of assistance in steering them in another direction.

As you can see, and accurate portrayal of the deceased plays a large part in the formation of a funeral message, so pay close attention to everything family members say about them, it might be the key to the message.

The Memorial Service

This is common in some areas, while not common in others, however it does serve a very useful purpose for some occasions. Sometimes, during family meetings, it becomes obvious that there are very many people who want to say something. Too many messages during a funeral service can detract from the service. More importantly to consider though, is that often funerals are conducted during working hours, and people take an early lunch to attend or take a vacation day. A funeral service that lasts over an hour, and if there are many speakers, can easily approach two hours, will result in people leaving before it concludes due to job constraints. Often these early departures can cause future conflict and hurt feelings, damaging relationships.

The memorial service is the perfect solution to this dilemma. It is held the night before, often at the funeral home and is scheduled for one hour, usually from 7-8 pm, with viewing an hour before. The casket is open and people, particularly family, are able to linger and say that long goodbye that is often very helpful to them.

The service itself is opened by the pastor with a brief prayer, followed by a brief reading from scripture and a short personal story about the deceased. Afterwards, a member of the family is called upon to share some memories, after which the microphone is announced as opened for any and all to say some words that may wish to. As the hour draws to a close, or if there is no one else who wishes to speak, the pastor once again takes the microphone and concludes the service with a brief prayer.

While the memorial service is not for all families, for families who have many who wish to say a few words, it has been a blessing to. From these families, I have heard nothing but compliments about how the memorial service gave them the room to say what they needed to say, and kept the funeral itself moving along nicely. I now make a point whenever I encounter a family that wants two, three or more speakers and multiple special songs to suggest taking these to a memorial service.

Scheduling

In preparation for the family meeting, the minister should already have prepared a copy of his church's schedule for the next 10 days. This allows you to confirm an acceptable date and time of the funeral, and memorial service if desired, at the meeting instead of having to follow up with the family. My practice is to clear the church schedule on the day requested if that is at all an option, to best minister to the needs of the family.

The most common times I have experienced are for the memorial service with viewing from 6-8 pm the night before the funeral, and the most common time for a funeral has been 11 am, with graveside following and a meal after that. While I am not rigid with these times, should the family not have discussed timing or remaining undecided, I suggest these, which are usually agreeable, because they are

the most common of times.

Family Conflict and Extreme Emotions

Throughout the funeral process, there are a lot of issues a minister must take into account to deliver a funeral experience that brings comfort, blessing and some degree of closure to the family of the deceased. Perhaps the most difficult of these issues to handle is family conflict. The other is one or more members of the family acting out in extreme emotions, usually during the service itself.

Family conflict can erupt during the planning stage and carry on long after the funeral is completed. Often it was already manifest, and the minister steps into it during the funeral process. Perhaps the best advice I could give for navigating sibling rivalry, for instance, is to not try to be the peacemaker to the bigger issues. Simply try to bring some sort of consensus on the order of service itself. Be willing to negotiate concessions from the opposing parties for peace's sake, but don't get involved any further, the timing isn't right to bring family counseling to the table.

I've found that offering the memorial service can placate bruised ego's or the more dramatic of members who are feeling left out of the service.

I have found it not uncommon for a family member or two to scream and wail during the service itself. A minister must know how to handle this professionally and not allow the service to spiral out of control, while at the same time allow for very real pain to be manifest. Usually, during the family meeting, you can identify who is most likely to act out in extreme emotions. Note also who among the family takes the comforting role.

If I see that one or two of the family members are reacting strongly during the planning meeting, I will make sure that I simply make mention of the room in the church we set apart for the family, and let them know that they are free to go there during the service if they feel they just can't handle the service. Proactive offering of the room saves many sanctuary dramas. It is also comforting to the family who often are embarrassed by extreme displays of emotion during the service.

I have found this to be the best way to handle emotions too strong for some to bear. It allows for minimal service disruption, and family know that if one of their members is very emotional, they have the pastor's permission to exit their seats and accompany the bereaved to a private room for mourning.

The Day of the Funeral

The day of the funeral, I arrive at the church early, and try to make sure everything is in operating order and fully prepared for the funeral. The day before I have delegated some people to prepare a room for the family. I make sure that it is ready and get the lights on. It is a good idea to have water, coffee and maybe some fresh fruit in this room. It is here that they will gather before the service for a final prayer and begin the family procession at the beginning of the service itself.

I also make sure the thermostat in the sanctuary is set to the proper temperature, unlock all exit doors and in general make sure everything on the church's end is taken care of before anyone else arrives. This is a good practice for all things regarding ministry in general. Make sure everything is taken care of before anyone else is there and you reduce the amount of surprises that can upset the best of intentions.

In my experience, for funerals scheduled for 11 am, they like to arrive around 9 am to properly position the casket for pre-service viewing and to arrange the floral displays, picture stands and guest book among their many responsibilities. So, all my pre-service checks should be completed by 8:45 am approximately. I have also found that it is not uncommon for family members to begin to arrive with the body, so readiness is important on my end.

The other people that arrive early is church volunteers. Many churches have people who are committed volunteers, and for funerals, they are often called upon to provide, or at least prepare, a post-service meal. For them it is good to see their pastor is already there and doors are unlocked as they arrive to offer their service to the bereaved. This also encourages and maintains healthy levels of volunteerism in the many areas a church needs volunteers in.

Conducting the Service

There are several things to keep in mind when officiated a funeral service. As I mentioned above, often funerals are scheduled during regular business hours, so attendees often take an early lunch or a half-day or full day off of work. With this in mind, punctuality is a must. Waiting around for one or two tardy people diminishes the experience of many who have come.

About 15 minutes before the service starts, I gather the family in the room the church has set apart for them. It is usually at this time that the funeral home likes to close the casket and move the casket to the front of the church, below the pulpit in preparation for the service. About 5 minutes before the starting time, I ask family to gather around and I say a brief prayer for them, and then I lead them out in procession to the sanctuary to their reserved seating, after which, I step to the pulpit to begin the service.

Welcome those who have gathered, and begin moving the service along in an orderly fashion. I believe that the best funeral services are no more than 45 minutes in length. If someone else giving the opening prayer, invite them to the pulpit and start right on time, moving the various elements of the service along in a steady flow.

When the time comes to give the message, I offer this advice. Above all things, pay attention to your audience and remain sensitive to the moment. Don't be afraid to shorten your message if you sense they are getting antsy, nor to further embellish a certain point should you have grabbed their attention. While normally I don't pay much attention to the clock while preaching, during this service I make sure my cell phone is out and frequently check the time.

When time draws near, wrap up the main points of the message and invite the one scheduled to make the closing prayer and any announcements up immediately.

I am providing some sample messages at the end of this book that I have preached in various funerals I have officiated.

When the service is dismissed, it is customary in many places for the officiating minister to lead the casket down the center aisle to the hearse waiting outside. Take your place, wait for the pallbearers and slowly, but not too slowly, lead the procession to the hearse, moving to your right, out of the way, as the pallbearers load the casket into

the hearse.

The Graveside

The transit to the graveside service is often immediately after the funeral service, though on occasion the family has requested that the meal is served first to accommodate those who have attended and then move on to the gravesite. Traditionally, though, it is right to the gravesite and then back to the church for a meal.

After the casket is loaded, the minister has two choices. The first is to ride in the hearse to the graveside, the second to drive their own car. I usually choose to drive myself, so I can return to the church earlier.

I have found that families prefer simple graveside services. Over the years, I've found that, no matter what the culture I am ministering in, simplicity brings the biggest blessing. This is because the graveside is an act of finality.

The way I have found most families prefer the graveside service is as follows:

- A brief opening prayer

- A simple reading of a traditional committal, including "ashes to ashes and dust to dust" that is no more than 5 minutes.

- The lowering of the coffin into the grave.

- Family members throwing a last rose on the casket.

- A recitation of The Lord's Prayer.

- A final prayer of committal and comfort.

- Some like to sing a favorite hymn or chorus while the first shovels of dirt are cast upon the casket, while others prefer to end the service after the closing prayer.

At this point, I talk to various people who have come out to the graveside and then make my way back to the church. Some family members want to linger at the graveside with other members, while others I have found move right back to the church for the meal. I simply respect those who want to linger privately and move on.

A Private Moment

Upon my arrival back to the church from the graveside, I go to my office and close the door for about 5 minutes. This is my time for myself. The funeral takes a great deal out of a minister, and I have found it to be very important to take these few minutes for myself, particularly if the deceased was a parishioner. When this is the case, I have suffered a loss as well, yet during the funeral process I have no place to shed a tear.

This is the time that I simply let myself shed a few tears, compose myself, take care of myself and move forward. Because I'm not a big crier, it usually is just a tear or two, but it is important, because I care about people, and I feel their loss when they die just like everyone else.

I encourage you to include these few moments in your funeral day for your own benefit, which will also be of benefit to those around you. You minister better when you take care of yourself as well.

The Meal

After taking my moment, and usually my tie off, I join the others at the meal, doing my best to greet as many people as possible. Basically, I play host and make sure everyone is taken care of.

I also include in my care the church volunteers. I want them to know that I appreciate the work that they do, their service to the members of the family who have suffered loss. I also check and see if they need help in any way. This blesses them, even if there isn't something I can do. Seeing their pastor willing to labor alongside and serve them in their service goes a long way, reaching every area of volunteerism in the church.

Sample Order of Service

This is the sample order of service that I take with me into the family meeting to give a bit of structure to preparing an order of service. I want to emphasize that this is not a rigid order of service, but rather something to get the conversation started and find out what the family really wants.

Order of Service

Greeting/Prayer:

Opening Congregational So Greeting/Prayer:

Special Song (Ideally Commemorative in Nature):

Eulogy/Obituary – Read by Family Member:

Brief Comments by family (If they desire a Family Statement):

Congregational Song (Ideally Healing/Comforting in Nature):

Brief Message:

Recitation of Lord's Prayer:

Closing Prayer and Announcements:

Using this sample order of service as the starting point, allow flexibility as the family desires, placing the names of each person who will perform each part. If they have other ministers who have played important roles in the spiritual life of the family, ideal places to place them are opening and closing prayers, along with leading The Lord's Prayer.

Sample Funeral Sermons

Below are a few sermon outlines that I've preached over the years. Feel free to use them as templates for your own services, just please don't claim them as your own. I pray they bless you and help you in the process.

This message was given at the funeral of a 45-year old single mother of 5 children who went to sleep in the night and never woke up.

Funeral Message – Single Mother

We are gathered here today to remember the life of Anna. Over the course of her life, she had overcome many things, and life looked to be really heading in the right direction when she unexpectedly passed away. She was so happy to have received her Bachelor's Degree and about her recent acceptance into a Master's Degree program.

I don't pretend to have answers to the question we are all asking, "Why did this have to happen, why now, when things were looking so good for the future?" I do know though, where to draw the strength to walk through this terrible loss.

Ps. 46:1 WEB
God is our refuge and strength,
    a very present help in trouble.

There isn't any other place, there isn't any other person that can be strong enough on their own at this time. Friends, family, people that have walked this road before you, they are all very important to lean on right now, but God is the ultimate source of strength, and He is willing to carry you through when you find you cannot carry yourself.

So the question would be then, how do I get this help from the Lord?

Ps. 121:1-2 WEB
I will lift up my eyes to the hills.
    Where does my help come from?
2 My help comes from Yahweh,

In these times of trouble, the way we receive strength from God is that we lift up our eyes to Him, we deliberately turn our hearts to Him, we acknowledge that He alone can be our strength. We choose simply to believe in Him and His promise that if we would turn our eyes to Him, He will grant to us the aid, the help the strength that is so desperately needed.

Scripture tells us that in our time, God has spoken to us through His Son, Jesus Christ.

Heb. 1:1-2 WEB
God, having in the past spoken to the fathers through the prophets at many times and in various ways, 2 has at the end of these days spoken to us by his Son, whom he appointed heir of all things, through whom also he made the worlds.

While we are gathered together today because of her death, I want to say a few brief words about life.

God's Son, Jesus Christ, told us that He came to bring us life.

John 10:10b WEB
I came that they may have life, and may have it abundantly.

Jesus came so that we who are still alive might truly experience living, life to the full. Jesus came to bring us abundant life. Salvation isn't about waiting around to die so that we can go to heaven; it is about living in heaven's life right now, here on earth. Eternal life doesn't begin when we die and go to heaven. Eternal life begins when we accept salvation, put our faith in Jesus and His work upon the cross as payment for our sin, what we often call being born again. God's desire is that all of humanity experiences eternal life, it is each of our ultimate purpose.

John 3:16-17 WEB
For God so loved the world, that he gave his one and only Son, that whoever believes in him should not perish, but have eternal life. 17 For God didn't send his Son into the world to judge the world, but that the world should be saved through him.

When we are born again, we enter into everlasting life. This is the life that Jesus was referring to when He said "I have come that they may have life, and that they may have it more abundantly."

Why would I say such a thing, that when we are born again we enter into everlasting life on this side of eternity? Jesus said

John 5:24 WEB
"Most certainly I tell you, he who hears my word, and believes him who sent me, has eternal life, and doesn't come into judgment, but has passed out of death into life.

We enter into life when we believe Him who was sent by the Father, Jesus Christ. When we believe in Jesus, we pass from death to life, life everlasting. When we believe in Jesus, we shall not come into judgment, but life.

This afternoon, I want to call you to eternal life, and that life begins the moment you receive Jesus Christ as your Lord and Savior. Make each chapter in the book of your life a chapter filled with the presence of God from this day forward.

Jesus is still inviting all who would call on His name, all who are gathered here this afternoon, to experience life abundantly, real life on this side of eternity, as Scripture says,

Heb. 3:15 WEB
while it is said, "Today if you will hear his voice, don't harden your hearts, as in the rebellion."

This message was given at the funeral of a dear old saint who had been the choir director for years at the church I currently pastor. She was diagnosed with cancer and died suddenly within the month.

Funeral Message – Older saint

We are gathered here today to remember the life of our sister.
I am so grateful to know that our Sister believed in Jesus. She loved Him and loved to praise Him. Music was such a big part of her life. From her choir directing to participation in the worship team for so many years, music, specifically music that lifted up the Name of Jesus was central to her life. This morning, I am assuming that I am addressing primarily the believers in Jesus Christ in this house.

The song that came to my mind in light of her passing was the song that I have asked the choir to sing directly before my message this morning, "One Day Jesus is Going to Call my Name". This is, you might say, is the title of my message this morning. Our Sister's passing was quick and decidedly unexpected. Her illness took her home so quickly. In many

ways, it reminded me of a parable that Jesus
gave found in

Luke 12:16-23 WEB
He spoke a parable to them, saying, "The
ground of a certain rich man produced
abundantly. 17 He reasoned within himself,
saying, 'What will I do, because I don't have
room to store my crops?' 18 He said, 'This is
what I will do. I will pull down my barns, and
build bigger ones, and there I will store all my
grain and my goods. 19 I will tell my soul,
"Soul, you have many goods laid up for many
years. Take your ease, eat, drink, be merry."'
20 "But God said to him, 'You foolish one,
tonight your soul is required of you. The things
which you have prepared—whose will they
be?' 21 So is he who lays up treasure for
himself, and is not rich toward God."
22 He said to his disciples, "Therefore I tell
you, don't be anxious for your life, what you will
eat, nor yet for your body, what you will wear.
23 Life is more than food, and the body is more
than clothing.

Those who put their faith in Christ first of all are
no fools. This is not the point of my message;
the point is the suddenness of the calling
home. One day Jesus is going to call our
names, and we do not know the day or the
hour any more than we know the day or the

hour of the coming of our Lord. We must live conscious of this fact, that should the Lord delay, should the final trumpet sound much later than we anticipate, we too shall breath our last and depart to our eternal reward, those who have put their faith in Jesus Christ as the final sacrifice for sin once and for all to eternal reward, those who have not believed to eternal punishment.

We make plans, we dream on this side of eternity, and I see nothing wrong with that, I do the same. Our culture is obsessed with retirement and the future. It seems the moment we enter the work force we're bombarded with retirement plans, 20-something and thinking about being 65 or 70, it's hard. We spend our working years worried about our 401k's, our investments, preparing for our elder years. If only we were so obsessed with our eternal retirement plan.

The point of the parable above is simple, our name is called at an unexpected moment. Our time on earth ends when we do not expect it to. The man in the parable was contemplating his retirement when his name was called. From my understanding of the story, he wasn't ready. His earthly retirement plan was a good one, and it was well supplied, but he didn't live to enjoy it, for his name was called. Today there are many people in this same situation, they have an ample earthly retirement plan, but their eternal retirement plan is bankrupt.

Christian, what is the state of your heavenly retirement account? Have you been investing for eternity? One day Jesus is going to call your name, are you living ready for that day?

The verses of this song speak of the ups and downs of life. Sometimes we're doing really well and other times we're doing really poorly. Sometimes we're proud of our walk with Christ and sometimes we're ashamed of our walk. But our goal is found in the chorus.

One day Jesus is going to call your name, it may be sooner, it may be later, but you cannot escape it, one day, your name will be called, and it matters today if you are ready for that call. The ultimate goal is that we get so close to Him, that it won't be a big change. Are you walking close to Him this morning?

The truth is, life is shorter than we want to believe it is. "What is your life? You are a mist, (a vapor), that appears for a little while and then vanishes' (James 4:14b) If we want to make the most of life, we need to face the fact that it is going to end." Sister Challenger was ready for the call, are you ready

Scripture tells us that in our time, God has spoken to us through His Son, Jesus Christ. God's Son, Jesus Christ, told us that He came to bring us real life, true life.

John 10:10b WEB
I came that they may have life, and may have it abundantly.

Jesus came so that we who are still alive might truly experience living, life to the full. Jesus came to bring us abundant life. Salvation isn't about waiting around to die so that we can go to heaven; it is about living in heaven's life right now, here on earth. Eternal life doesn't begin when we die and go to heaven. Eternal life begins when we accept salvation, put our faith in Jesus and His work upon the cross as payment for our sin, what we often call being born again. God's desire is that all of humanity experiences eternal life, it is each of our ultimate purpose.

John 3:16-17 WEB
For God so loved the world, that he gave his one and only Son, that whoever believes in him should not perish, but have eternal life. 17 For God didn't send his Son into the world to judge the world, but that the world should be saved through him.

When we are born again, we enter into everlasting life. This is the life that Jesus was referring to when He said "I have come that they may have life, and that they may have it more abundantly." Why would I say such a thing, that when we are born again we enter into everlasting life on this side of eternity? Jesus said

John 5:24 WEB
"Most certainly I tell you, he who hears my word, and believes him who sent me, has eternal life, and doesn't come into judgment, but has passed out of death into life.

We enter into life when we believe Him who was sent by the Father, Jesus Christ. When we believe in Jesus, we pass from death to life, life everlasting. When we believe in Jesus, we shall not come into judgment, but life.

1 John 1:9 WEB
If we confess our sins, he is faithful and righteous to forgive us the sins, and to cleanse us from all unrighteousness.

This morning, I want to call you to eternal life, and that life begins the moment you receive Jesus Christ as your Lord and Savior. Jesus is still inviting all who would call on His name, all who are gathered here this afternoon, to experience life abundantly, real life on this side of eternity, as Scripture says,

Heb. 3:15 WEB
while it is said, "Today if you will hear his voice, don't harden your hearts, as in the rebellion."

I pray that these sermons are of value to you as you seek to minister comfort and the Word of God to those who are grieving in your ministry at this time.

CPSIA information can be obtained
at www.ICGtesting.com
Printed in the USA
BVHW030822300419
546934BV00001B/51/P

9 781522 028901